# UNFORGETTABLE ELEPHANT JOKES

D1092606

KINGFISHER

Why do elephants want to be alone?
*Because two's a crowd.*

What's grey and moves at
a hundred miles an hour?
*A jet-propelled*
*elephant.*

What's big and grey and wears a mask?
*The Elephantom of the Opera.*

What's grey with red spots?
*An elephant with the measles.*

What's grey and never needs ironing?
*A drip-dry elephant.*

What's big and red and grey?
*A sunburnt elephant.*

What is grey, stands in a river during a storm and doesn't get wet?
*An elephant with an umbrella.*

What's grey and goes round and round?
*An elephant in a washing machine.*

What's grey and powdery?
*Instant elephant mix.*

What's grey and highly dangerous?
*An elephant with a machine gun.*

What's big and grey and lives in Scotland?
*The Loch Ness Elephant.*

What's yellow on the outside and grey on the inside?
*An elephant disguised as a banana.*

What's big and grey and protects you from the rain?
*An umbrellaphant.*

What's grey, wrinkly and has sixteen wheels?
*An elephant on roller-skates.*

What's big, grey and flies straight up?
*An elecopter.*

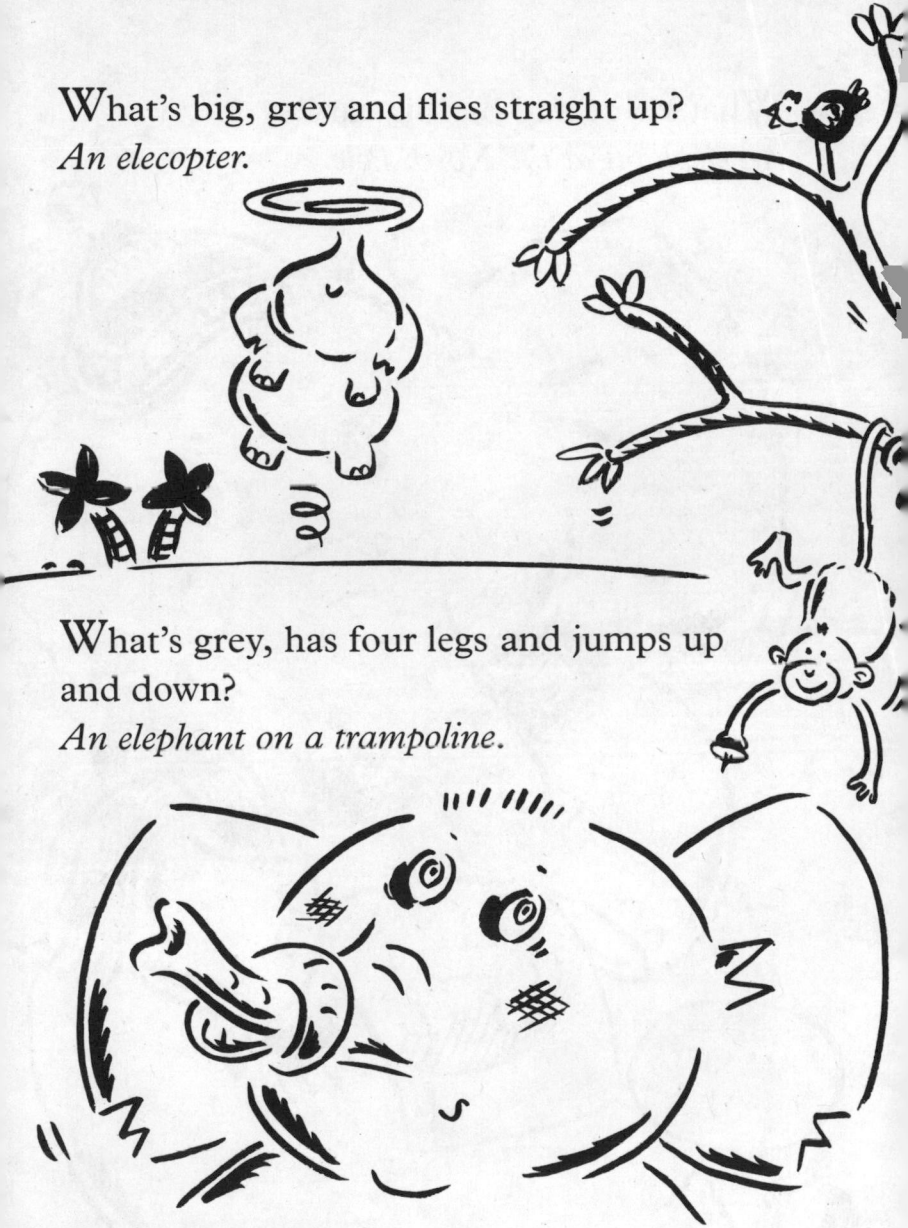

What's grey, has four legs and jumps up and down?
*An elephant on a trampoline.*

What's bright red and weighs four tonnes?
*An elephant holding its breath.*

What's blue and has big ears?
*An elephant at the North Pole.*

What's grey and wrinkly and jumps every twenty seconds?
*An elephant with hiccups.*

restaurant / bar

stock room

What has three tails, seven feet and four trunks?
*An elephant with spare parts.*

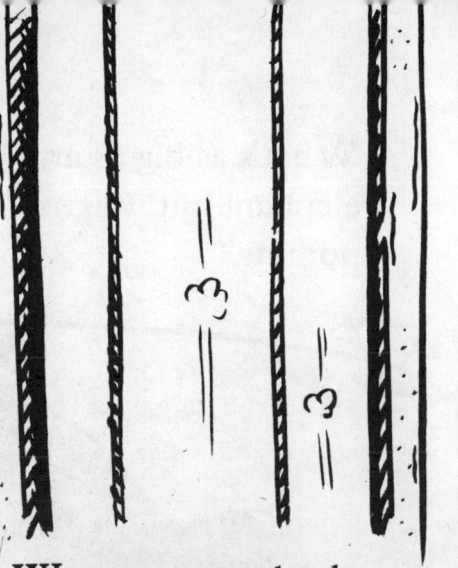

What goes up slowly but comes down fast?
*An elephant in a lift.*

What's as big as an elephant but weighs nothing?

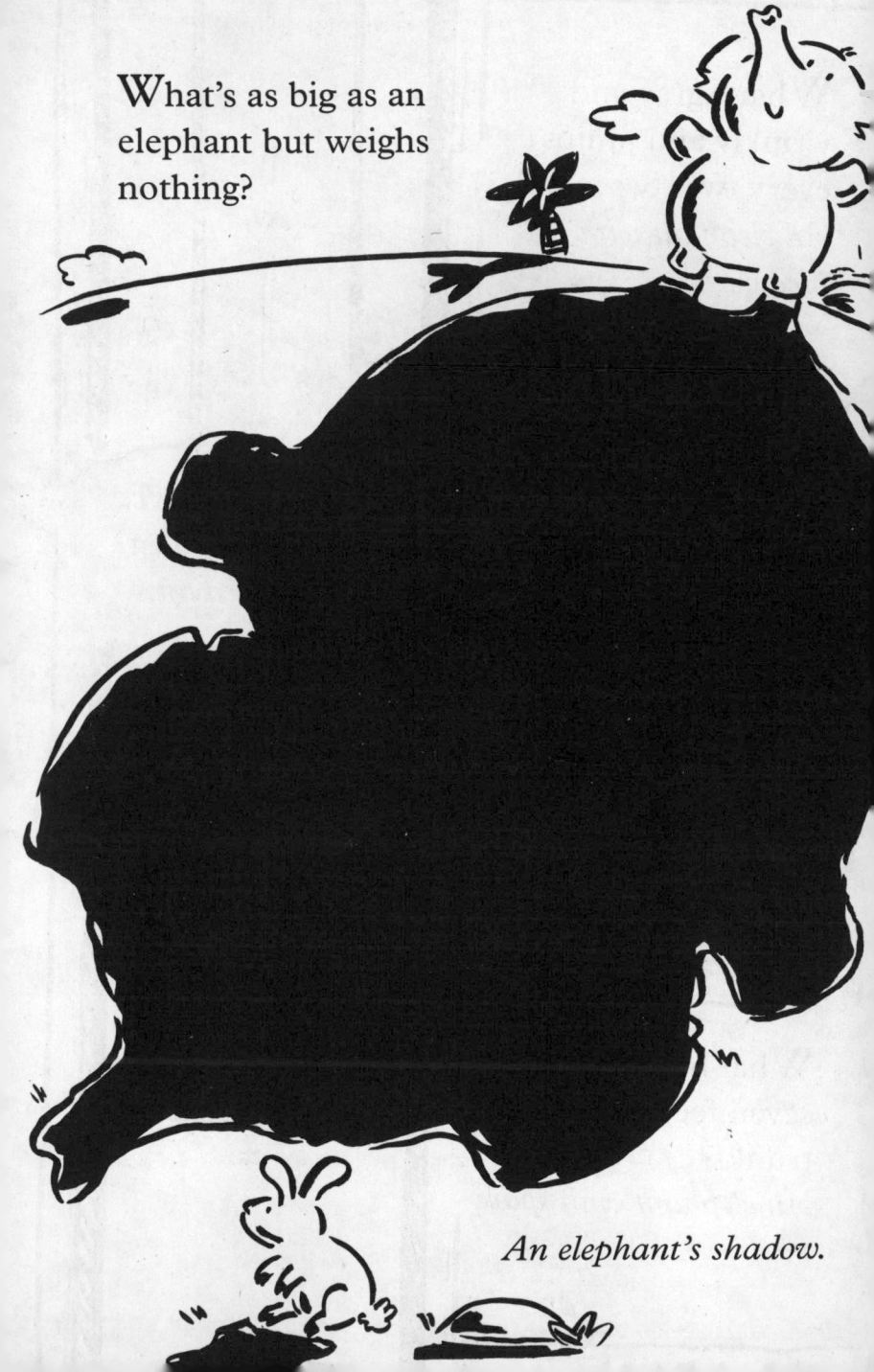

*An elephant's shadow.*

What's grey and lights up?
*An electric elephant.*

What's grey but turns red?
*An embarrassed elephant.*

What's grey, carries a bunch of flowers, and cheers you up when you're ill?
*A Get-wellephant.*

What's big and grey with horns?
*An elephant marching band.*

What's grey, has a wand, huge wings, and gives money to elephants?
*The Tusk fairy.*

What's grey, beautiful and wears glass slippers?
*Cinderelephant.*

What's the difference between an injured elephant and bad weather?

*One roars with pain, the other pours with rain.*

FRED: What's the difference between an elephant and a postbox?

BERT: I don't know.

FRED: Well, I'm not sending you to post my letters.

What's the difference between an elephant and a bad pupil?
*One rarely bites, the other barely writes.*

How do you tell the difference between a mouse and an elephant?
*Try picking them up!*

What's the difference between an elephant and a piece of paper?
*You can't make a paper aeroplane out of an elephant.*

What's the difference between a sick elephant and seven days?

*One is a weak one, the other is one week.*

What's the difference between an elephant and a banana?

*Have you ever tried to peel an elephant?*

What's the difference between an elephant and a gooseberry?

*A gooseberry is green.*

Why are elephants grey?
*So you can tell them from flamingoes.*

What's the difference between an elephant and a flea?
*An elephant can have fleas but a flea can't have elephants.*

What's the difference between an African and an Indian elephant?
*About three thousand miles.*

What's worse than an elephant with a sore trunk?
*A centipede with sore feet.*

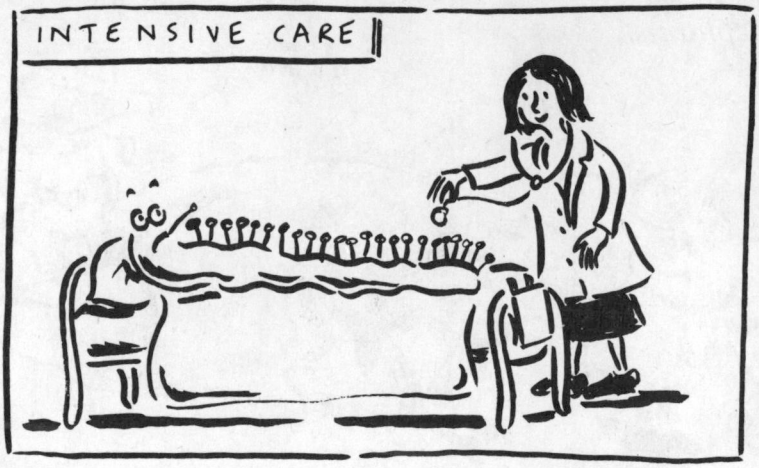


Why is an elephant large, grey and wrinkled?
*Because if it was small, white and round it would be an aspirin.*

ELEPHANT KEEPER: "My elephant's not well. Do you know a good animal doctor?"

ZOO KEEPER: "No, I'm afraid all the doctors I know are people."

PATIENT: Doctor, doctor, I keep seeing pink and yellow elephants.

DOCTOR: Have you seen a psychiatrist?

PATIENT: No, only pink and yellow elephants.

Why do elephants scratch themselves?
*Because they're the only ones who know where they itch.*

ELEPHANT: "Doctor, I've lost my memory!"
DOCTOR: "When did this happen?"
ELEPHANT: "When did what happen?"

Why is a sneezing elephant like a spy?
*They both have a code in the head.*

What pills do you give an elephant that can't sleep?
*Trunkquillizers.*

A boy with an elephant on his head went to see a doctor. The doctor said, "You know, you really need help."

*"Yes I do,"* the elephant cried, *"get this kid off my foot!"*

What kind of elephants live in Antarctica?
*Cold ones.*

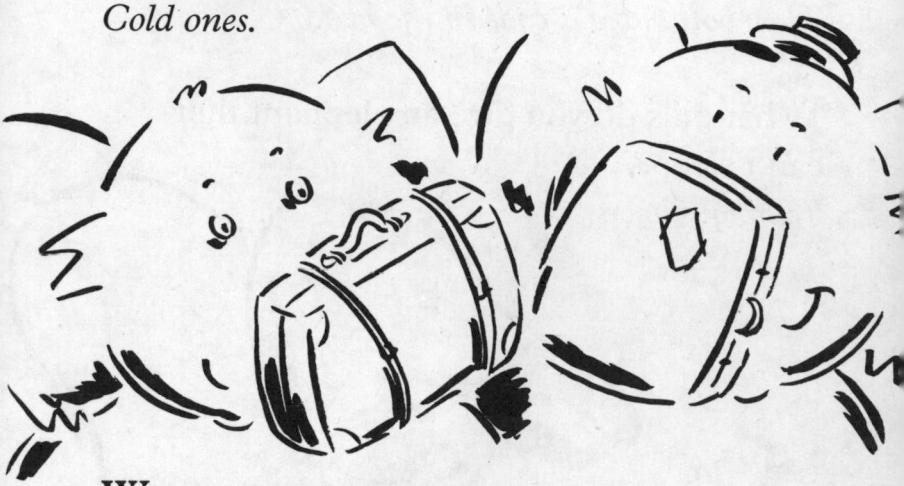

Why do elephants have trunks?
*Because they'd look silly carrying suitcases.*

How do you get five elephants into a small car?
*Two in the back, two in the front and one in the glove compartment.*

How does an elephant get out of a small car?
*The same way he got in.*

Why did the elephant cross the road?
*Because the chicken was having a day off.*

What do you call an elephant at the North Pole?
*Lost.*

Which takes less time to get ready for a trip, an elephant or a rooster?
*A rooster - he only takes his comb.*

What did the hotel manager say to the elephant who couldn't pay his bill?
*"Pack your trunk and clear out."*

How do you get an elephant into a matchbox?
*Take all the matches out first.*

What happened to the elephant who ran away with the circus?
*The police made him bring it back!*

Why shouldn't you take an elephant to a zoo?
*Because he'd rather go to the movies.*

How can you tell if an elephant has been in your fridge?
*Footprints in the butter.*

What did the grape say when the elephant stepped on it?
*Nothing. It just let out a wine.*

EXOTIC
PET SHOP
ELEPHANT
FOR SALE
Will Eat Anything –
Very Fond of Children

How do you know if there's an elephant in your dessert?
*You get very lumpy ice cream!*

"I know an elephant who lives on garlic alone."
*"I'm not surprised he lives alone if all he eats is garlic."*

Why are elephants wiser than chickens?
*Ever heard of Kentucky Fried Elephant?*

Why do elephants eat raw food?
*Because they don't know how to cook.*

Have you heard about the elephant who went on a crash diet?
*He wrecked a bus, three cars and a fire engine.*

Why did the elephant eat candles?
*For light refreshment.*

What do you do with a green elephant?
*Wait until it ripens.*

Why did the elephant sleep in a bowl of salad dressing?
*So he'd wake up really oily.*

What do invisible elephants drink?
*Evaporated milk.*

When should you feed elephant milk to a baby?
*When it's a baby elephant.*

If you were making an omelette would you choose chicken eggs or elephant eggs?
*Chicken eggs because elephant yolks are usually terrible!*

An elephant walked into a cafe and ordered a strawberry milkshake. He drank it in one gulp, paid and left.

The customers in the cafe couldn't believe their eyes. One of them said to the waitress, "What an amazing elephant! Has he done that before?"

"Oh, no," said the waitress. "Normally he has a small coke."

How do you know peanuts are fattening?

*Have you ever seen a skinny elephant?*

What do you call an elephant that can't do sums?
*Dumbo.*

"My elephant plays chess with me."

"How amazing! It must be a really intelligent animal."

"Not really. I've won three games to two so far today."

JIM: "My homework's really difficult tonight – I've got to write an essay on the elephant."

JOHN: "Well, for a start, you're going to need a very big ladder . . ."

Why do elephants do well in school?

*Because they have a lot of grey matter.*

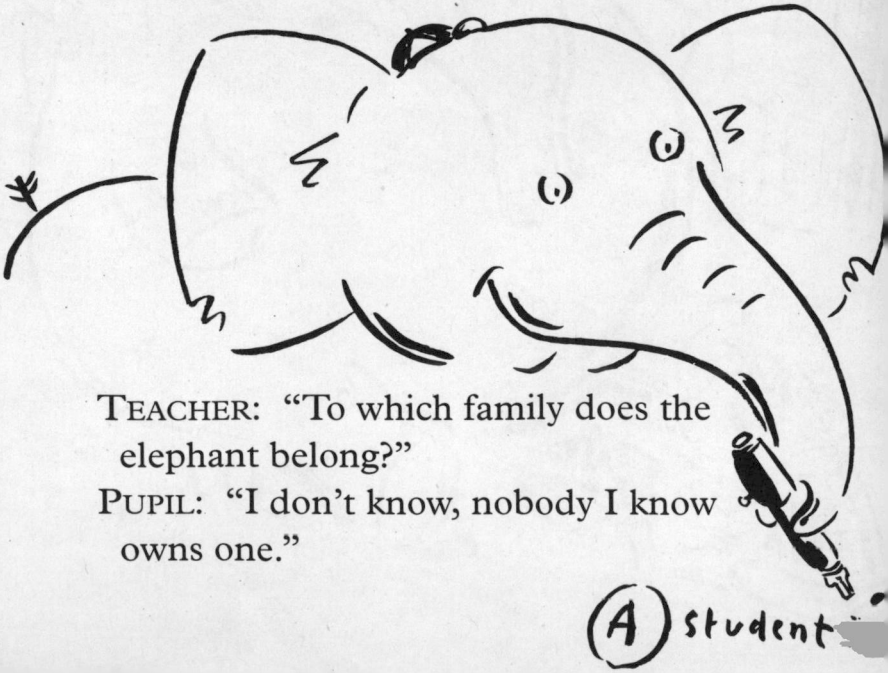


TEACHER: "To which family does the elephant belong?"

PUPIL: "I don't know, nobody I know owns one."

"How do you spell elephant?"

"E-l-l-e-e-f-a-n-t."

"That's not how the dictionary spells it."

"You didn't ask me how the dictionary spelt it."

TEACHER: "Name six wild animals."

PUPIL: "Two lions and four elephants."

TEACHER: "Where would you find an elephant?"

PUPIL: "You don't have to find them – they're too big to lose."

d when he came home.
you been doing?" asked Jane.
herd of elephants on vines."
said Jane. "I thought elephants
the ground."

Why shouldn't you go into the jungle at midday?

*Because that's when elephants practise parachuting.*

What is an easy way to get a wild elephant?

*Buy a tame one and annoy it.*

What did Tarzan say when he saw the elephants coming?
*"Here come the elephants!"*

What's the best way to see a charging herd of elephants?
*On television!*

Why don't elephants like playing cards in the jungle?
*Because of all the cheetahs.*

What do you call an elephant that never washes?
*A smellyphant.*

What do you call an elephant with a carrot in each ear?
*Anything, he can't hear you.*

What do you call an elephant with a machine gun?
*Sir!*

What can an elephant with a machine gun call you?
*Anything he likes!*

What do you call an elephant that's small and pink?
*A failure.*

What do you call an elephant who lies across the middle of a tennis court?
*Annette!*

What do you call an elephant creeping through the jungle in the middle of the night?
*Russell!*

What do you call an elephant with a seagull on its head?
*Cliff!*

What do you call an elephant with a rabbit up its sweater?
*Warren!*

What do you call the rabbit up the elephant's sweater?
*Terrified!*

What do you call someone with an elephant on their head?
*Squashed.*

How do elephants speak to each other?
*By 'elephone.*

What did the zoo keeper say when he saw three elephants in sunglasses coming over a hill?
*Nothing, he didn't recognize them.*

When do elephants have eight feet?
*When there are two of them.*

How can you tell when there's an elephant under the bed?

*When you're nearly touching the ceiling.*

What do you give an elephant with big feet?
*Plenty of room.*

What do you say when an elephant sits on your sofa?

*It's time to get a new sofa!*

Why did the elephant walk on two legs?

*To give the ants a chance.*

Why do elephants have trunks?
*Because they have no pockets to put things in.*

A man was sprinkling white powder on his lawn.

"Why are you doing that?" asked his neighbour.

"It's to keep the elephants off the grass," replied the first man.

"But we don't get any elephants around here!"

"I know – good stuff, isn't it?"

Which animals were the last to leave the ark?
*The elephants, because they had to pack their trunks.*

What would happen if an elephant sat in front of you at the movies?
*You would miss most of the film.*

What steps would you take if you were being chased by an elephant?
*Big ones.*

What do you find in an elephant's graveyard?
*Elephantoms.*

Why do elephants have wrinkly ankles?
*Because their shoes are too tight.*

Which is stronger, an elephant or a snail?
*A snail, because it carries its house. An elephant only carries its trunk.*

What do you do with old cannon balls?
*Give them to elephants to use as marbles.*

What do elephants do in the evenings?
*Watch elevision.*

Who lost a herd of elephants?
*Big Bo Peep.*

What is an elephant's favourite film?
*Elephantasia.*

What did the elephant say to the famous detective?
*It's ele-mentary, my dear Sherlock.*

ZOO KEEPER: "I've lost one of my elephants."
OTHER ZOO KEEPER: "Why don't you put an advertisement in the paper?"
ZOO KEEPER: "Don't be silly, he can't read."

What do you do if you find a blue elephant?
*Try to cheer it up.*

Why did the elephant jump in the lake when it began to rain?

*To stop getting wet.*

What is a baby elephant after he is five weeks old?
*Six weeks old.*

What did the elephant say when the man grabbed him by the tail?
*This is the end of me.*

POLICEMAN: "One of your elephants has been seen chasing a man on a bicycle."

ZOO KEEPER: "Nonsense. None of my elephants know how to ride a bicycle."

Why are elephants wrinkled all over?

*Because they don't fit on an ironing board.*

What do you get if you cross a parrot with an elephant?
*An animal that tells you everything it remembers.*

What do elephants sing at Christmas?
*No-elephants, No-elephants . . .*

Who do elephants get their Christmas presents from?
*Elephanta Claus!*

How do you hire an elephant?
*Stand it on four bricks.*

"Dad! Mum is fighting with an enormous elephant in the front garden!"

"Don't worry, dear, I'm sure the elephant can look after itself."

"I say, I say, I say, my elephant's
got no trunk."
"How does he smell?"
"Terrible!"

How are elephants and
hippopotamuses alike?
*Neither can play basketball.*

How do you keep an angry elephant from charging?

*Take away his credit cards.*

What did the baby elephant get when the daddy elephant sneezed?

*Out of the way!*

Why do elephants have short tails?
*They can't remember long stories.*

How do you keep an elephant in suspense?
*I'll tell you tomorrow.*

Why is an elephant braver than a hen?
*Because the elephant isn't chicken.*

What's worse than raining cats and dogs?
*Raining elephants.*

What should you do if an elephant breaks down your front door?

*Escape through the back door.*

How do you raise a baby elephant that has been abandoned by its parents?

*With a fork-lift truck.*

FATHER: "I'd like an elephant for my son, please."
PET SHOP OWNER: "I'm sorry, sir, we don't do swops."

Why was the elephant wearing red shoes?
*Because her black ones were at the menders.*

## Other titles in the *Sidesplitters* series you might enjoy:

0 7534 0987 9

0 7534 0986 0

0 7534 0990 9

0 7534 0985 2